ORGANIZING
FOR
AGRICULTURAL
DEVELOPMENT

ORGANIZING
FOR
AGRICULTURAL
DEVELOPMENT

**Human Aspects in the Utilization of
Science and Technology**

by

William Foote Whyte

ta

Transaction Books
New Brunswick, New Jersey

To Kathleen

Contents

Contents

Acknowledgments

For their helpful criticisms and suggestions concerning the ideas presented here, I am particularly indebted to the following people: Randolph Barker, Milton Barnett, Stillman Bradfield, John M. Cohen, E.W. Coward, Luis Deustua, Matthew Drosdoff, Milton Esman, Douglas Horton, Gilbert Levine, Daisy Núñez del Prado, Ulises Moreno, Robert L. Plaisted, Maria Mayer de Scurrah, Luis Soberon, H.D. Thurston, Michael Twomey, Norman Uphoff, and Frank Young. Of course, they are not responsible for the views expressed here.

This book was prepared for Cornell University's Program for Policies for Science and Technology in Developing Nations, which is supported by the Agency for International Development.

Introduction

As new problems are recognized in the wake of spectacular successes, we find ourselves in a period of reevaluation of the significance of the green revolution. This provides an opportune moment for rethinking the role of the behavioral scientist in agricultural and rural development.[1] My aim is to review what is known of the problems and possibilities of agricultural and rural development, to diagnose the deficiencies in behavioral scientists' efforts to contribute in this field in the past and to present an organizational framework designed to advance both theory and practice.

The ideas presented here are based upon a 10-year program of research on changes in Peruvian rural communities, carried out jointly by the Institute of Peruvian Studies and Cornell University, supplemented by scattered interviews and discussions with agricultural scientists working with national and international agencies concerned with rural research and development and with government officials responsible for progress in agriculture.

In sorting out the ideas gained from experience and reading in rural development, I have come to recognize important parallels in the evolution of knowledge in this field when it is compared with organizational behavior (also known as industrial sociology, bureaucratic organizations, etc.), a field in which I began working in 1942. Ideas in the two fields are in the process of reformulation along such parallel lines as to suggest that explicit recognition of these intellectual trends can serve to clarify and strengthen future work in agricultural development. In the final section of this book, I shall draw the parallels and explore their implications.

Achievements and Limitations of the Green Revolution

Early reports of research and development in international research centers made it clear that genuine scientific breakthroughs were being achieved. Such reports evoked enthusiasm throughout the world. It seemed that the new miracle seeds, combined with new methods of cultivation, were going to solve two of the basic problems of humanity. They promised to eliminate the threatened scarcities of foods and to raise the standard of living of farmers of the Third World.

It was not usually the scientists themselves who made these glowing predictions; they spoke with appropriate caution of the limitations of their work and of the serious problems still to be solved. Nevertheless, the production potential of the new seeds was so far beyond anything previously available that reporters in the media wrote of eventual possibilities as if they were on the threshhold of achievement. Even behavioral scientists were overawed by the accomplishments of their colleagues in the agricultural sciences. Could it be that the new seed varieties offered such large potential rewards to farmers as to overcome the traditional peasant "resistance to change," thus eliminating one of our favorite topics of research?

To understand the limitations as well as the potentialities of the green revolution, we must distinguish between the production of food and the economic welfare of the food producers. In production, spectacular results have indeed been achieved with some crops in some areas of some countries. In terms of the welfare of the producers, results have been mixed. While in some areas small farmers have benefited, the chief beneficiaries have been large- and medium-sized farmers.

Why this concentration of benefits? Taking advantage of the new seeds and new methods of cultivation requires increased expenditures on seeds, fertilizers and other inputs, plus the availability of an ample water supply. The small farmer generally lacks the money to purchase the new input package, and low-cost credit is not generally available to him. If the farmer does not have access to irrigation water and must depend upon rainfall, the most impressive advances of the green revolution are beyond his reach. Even having land within an irrigation system does not guarantee that the small farmer will receive the water necessary for green revolution technology. In many cases, small farmers are on the margin of irrigation systems, and whenever water is in short supply the larger and more politically powerful farmers receive a disproportionate share of the water so that the shortages fall particularly upon the small holders. This problem of inequities becomes more acute as the big farmers adopt innovations that increase their demand for water. Furthermore, an irrigation system that previously provided enough water for all its members may not be adequate to meet the new conditions. Large farmers can bring in subsurface water through investing in tube wells and pumping systems and find that the increased productivity of land more than pays the increased investment. Small farmers acting individually may find their property too small to profit from this type of investment and the fixed cost it involves.

Several studies have shown that in certain areas the introduction of the new technology and farming methods has actually damaged the interests of the rural lower class.[2] As the more prosperous farmers increase their income with the new inputs, they may increasingly mechanize their farms, thus reducing their needs for hired labor. As they find direct operation of their farms more profitable under the new conditions, they may seek to push share-croppers out. In contrast, a recent report on the effects of introduction of the new rice varieties in a number of Asian countries[3] suggests that in some areas "the labor-displacing effects the labor-saving practices had were more than offset by the increased labor requirement of the pre-harvest labor tasks."

Since the effects of the new technologies will be strongly affected by the land tenure system and the social structure and distribution of power in the local area and by government agricultural development programs and policies, no global generalizations about the impact of the green revolution upon the rural lower class can be fully accurate. Yet the differential impact of the green revolution up to this point is a well-established fact; whether or not the rural poor have actually become poorer through these changes, the benefits of the green revolution have gone predominantly to the more prosperous farmers.

This conclusion has led to a redefinition of the problem of agricultural and rural development in the Third World. The "trickle down" theory of progress has been discredited. We no longer assume that, if the "good farmers" (meaning the larger, wealthier and better educated producers) achieve success with the innovations, the "demonstration effect" will lead the small and poor farmers to follow their example. Structural barriers block the flow of innovation from the research institute to poor farmers at the bottom of the rural social structure.

We are now recognizing that overall growth in the gross national product does not necessarily contribute to raising the standard of living of the poorest segment of the population of the Third World. The fruits of the advances of science and technology are generally appropriated by the already rich and powerful. This conclusion is no longer

limited to the field of academic research. Robert Mc-
Namara, president of the World Bank, has pointed out
repeatedly that, in many countries in the developing
world, the poorest segment of the population (some 40
percent at the lower income levels) has not improved its
income despite very satisfactory percentage increases in
total GNP from year to year.

The McNamara doctrine is now so well established that
it is official policy of the Agency for International Development to limit its projects for rural and agricultural development to those that are designed to have a favorable impact upon the small farmer. While there is no guarantee
that such projects will achieve their objectives, at least it
is clear that AID officials have abandoned the "trickle
down" theory.

There is now increasing recognition, even among the
hardest-nosed agricultural scientists, that progress in
technology and in the scientific fields directly related to
the growth of plants is necessary but not sufficient to
produce major social and economic benefits. The agricultural scientists are increasingly turning to the behavioral
scientists to ask: "What is to be done now?"

How are we to reply to this challenge? For years we
have been complaining that the agricultural scientists
were not listening to the wisdom we claimed to offer regarding culture, social structure and economic processes,
but at least in that situation we bore no responsibility for
the failures of agricultural development efforts. Now, if
the agricultural scientists are really seeking our advice
and collaboration, we shall have to accept the challenge of
responsibility

2

Recognition of Behavioral Science Deficiencies

If behavioral scientists are to respond to this challenge, we should do so in a spirit of humility, recognizing the deficiencies that have existed in our fields in meeting the demands for social and economic knowledge of rural development. It is customary to phrase this humble spirit in terms of the recognition that the "hard" sciences are much farther advanced than the behavioral sciences. While this general statement is true enough, it represents a misdiagnosis of the problem. The problem is not simply the slow pace of learning; the problem is that some of the most widely held beliefs of behavioral scientists have turned out to be dead wrong. Only as we recognize these past errors will we have a chance to find a new direction that will contribute to agricultural and rural development.

One of the behavioral scientists' most cherished beliefs is what I call "the myth of the passive peasant." According to this myth, the peasant is, by his very nature, passive, fatalistic, tradition bound and resistant to change. This myth is a convenient rationalization for the change agent who has failed to propel the peasants into action. By placing the blame upon the resistance to change that "everybody knows" prevails in the peasant community, he can escape personal responsibility for his failure.

While behavioral scientists have not needed such an excuse, they have accepted the myth nevertheless. Representative of the general view prevailing in the recent past is the following statement drawn from a report of a prestigious interdisciplinary group discussing rural social change strategies:

> The behavioral scientists had their various special diagnoses, but were, after the habit of their kind, less positive as to solutions. They accused the first two groups (agronomists and economists) of neglecting the special values held by the traditional peasant and overrating the importance of technical knowledge and economic incentives. The rural villager, they said, is a prisoner of his culture and his history, suspicious of change or innovation, not accustomed to taking the risks involved in producing for a market, and is, therefore, differently motivated from the commercial farmer. They tended to take the gloomy view that there was not much hope until the whole structure of rural society was rather radically altered and its values changed through fundamental education, a breakup of the extended family, and the spread of mass communications.[4]

The persistence of this belief is especially hard to understand in Peru, where the peasants have provided ample evidence of indigenously organized change efforts in recent years. In the 1950s and 1960s, peasant movements have transformed large areas of rural Peru.[5] In a number of communities, major changes in crops planted and in methods of cultivation that have been very largely brought about by the initiative and drive of the peasants themselves have been documented.[6] To be sure, such changes did not take place in what have been called in the literature "closed peasant communities." While there are wide variations among communities in Peru regarding their openness or closedness to the outside world, it would be difficult to find a community completely cut off from outside influences. In some cases, changes have been introduced by young men who returned to the community after months or years of migratory experience that exposed them to new types of agricultural knowledge. In two cases, schoolteachers provided essential stimuli and links to the outside world of agricultural methods and resources, and in one of these cases the teachers had all been born and brought up in the rural community, although, of course, they had gone out for several years to complete their own educations.

In such cases, agricultural extension agents have indeed played a role, but it has not been the classic change agent role of the outsider who diagnoses the problems and gets a passive community into motion. While sometimes an extension agent has taken the intiative, we find that small farmers seek out the extension man in pursuit of information needed for carrying out changes they themselves have set in motion. We have even found cases where members of a rural community have by-passed the extension service and gone directly to the agrarian university, where they assume that the knowledge they need is being produced.

One factor that has prevented behavioral scientists from recognizing peasant activism, which has been so prevalent in Peru (and probably in other Third World countries), has been our unquestioning faith in the knowledge of agricultural scientists. Unconsciously we have assumed that extension agents get this certified knowledge from the agricultural scientist and pass it on to the peasant. If the peasant declines to accept and apply this knowledge, it cannot be for rational reasons and therefore it must be because he is fatalistic, tradition bound and guided by superstitions. It has not occurred to us that what has been offered might in some cases be simply bad advice, in which case the peasant would be well advised to simulate the passivity that the extensionist has come to expect of him. (In Peruvian communities it has not been customary for small farmers to express openly any disagreement with higher status and better educated persons. The safe re-

sponse has been one of apparent but passive acquiescence
as long as the higher status person is around.)

Recently I have begun to hear of cases illustrating the
fallibility of expert advice in agriculture. For a time I set
about collecting stories in which small farmers encountered disaster upon accepting the recommendations of extension agents. These cases tend not to be reported in the
literature for obvious reasons, but once we begin looking
for them we can quickly build up a file of examples from
various parts of the world. There seems no need to reveal
what is in my small but growing file, for the fallibility of
the extension agent is coming to be increasingly recognized, as the following two examples will indicate.

James Green[7] reported on an AID training program
designed to improve the abilities of extension agents in
Pakistan. The program emphasized group discussion,
field work and practice demonstrations of the skills agents
were trying to transmit to farmers. Green and his as-
sociates encountered particular difficulties at the point
where the agents were asked to go beyond the writing of
lesson plans and the description of skills to the actual
demonstration before the class of a skill chosen by each
agent.

> The first two [steps] required only verbal skills, but the
> demonstration required an ability to perform the skill,
> step by step, with a degree of proficiency gained only
> through considerable experience. The panic resulted in
> attempts to have the advisor-instructors assume the re-
> sponsibility of selection. When this failed, a number of
> the participants let down all barriers and confessed to
> the advisor-assistant teachers that they did not feel
> confident enough of their ability to demonstrate a single
> skill in their own technical field! The explanation was
> simple: they themselves had been trained in a lecture
> system and had never performed the skill, or had done
> so only once or twice. There were veterinarians who
> had never castrated a bull calf; animal husbandry men
> who had never culled poultry; horticulturists who had

never pruned a tree; extension-methods educators who had never organized any kind of activity, club or council in the village, etc.

It is often claimed that professional men in Latin America and other parts of the developing world are handicapped in their efforts to communicate with lower class people because "getting their hands dirty" is beneath their dignity. Since social mobility depends upon education and higher education is so heavily oriented toward oral and written communication, this identification of dirty work with low status is natural, but Green's report points to a deeper obstacle to good communication across status levels. Probably many of these professionals could be persuaded that it was a good idea to get their hands dirty if they had any confidence in what they were supposed to do with those hands. A man who lacks such confidence naturally prefers to be considered a snob rather than a fool.

The same theme is explored further in a recent study of adult education in rural areas around the world.

The urgency of upgrading the knowledge of extension agents was dramatically demonstrated by the results of diagnostic tests given by IRRI (International Rice Research Institute) to several thousand extension workers, extension supervisors and highly trained agricultural experts. The purpose was to assess their ability to identify such things as common pests, diseases and nutritional problems of the rice plant, and to prescribe appropriate chemical treatments for them. On the average, only 25 percent of the questions were answered correctly by extension supervisors and workers from rice producing areas. The more highly trained agricultural experts did no better. An IRRI official concluded:

Whatever the reasons, and these vary with conditions, the typical extension worker in most Southeast Asian countries lacks background knowledge of rice culture and has had little or no first-hand paddy experience. Moreover, when he lacks the necessary diagnostic skills, he cannot identify the problems in the farmer's field and thus cannot advise him on appropriate action. Consequently, he is reluctant even to approach the farmer to show him how things might be done. [8]

I am not suggesting that the agricultural professionals are always or usually wrong. Their advice may well be useful more often than not. All I am trying to demonstrate with these examples is that the "expert" is not always right and that "resistance to change" on the part of peasants may be a rational response to poor advice. Discovering cases where peasants have declined to follow the advice of the experts provides us with no proof of peasants' inherent traditionalism and fatalism.

Another major source of error in the behavioral sciences lies in the research design generally found in studies of the diffusion of innovation. Since it is much easier to follow the spread of a single innovation, diffusion researchers have tended to concentrate on *the* innovation, whether it be the use of a new type of seed, fertilizer or a new cropping practice.

We have come to recognize the insufficiency of any single change. In agriculture, it is very rare indeed that a sole innovation produces a substantial improvement in the standard of living of the peasants. Even in changes so impressive as those growing out of the green revolution, the impact of the new seed may depend upon the farmer's ability to acquire the fertilizer and insecticides he needs, to improve his access to irrigation water and to get accurate and timely information needed for the efficient utilization of the new farming methods. [9] Furthermore, the small farmer will need credit for financing the purchase of the new inputs and a market price for his crop high enough to reward him for the additional time and money expended in adopting the new methods.

3

An Organizational Framework for Studies of Agricultural Development

In a field so multifaceted as agricultural development, we need to develop a framework to provide a useful context for facts, theoretical interpretations and speculative ideas. I propose to build such a framework upon *organizational relations* and *information flows*.

Why speak of "information" rather than "knowledge"? Knowledge implies systematic bodies of validated data and relationships in particular disciplines. Information is a more inclusive term, covering not only formal knowledge but also where to go to find something out, who has done what and with what result, who has the money to support what project and so on. By the use of the term, I do not limit myself to validated information, and yet I find the common dichotomy between information and misinformation an oversimplification. The people who generate, transmit or receive information develop ways of judging both the accuracy of the information and its relevance for their purposes. At some points information may be validated (or invalidated) through scientific tests, at other points it may be evaluated in terms of the reputation of the transmitter or in terms of the reactions of influential others in the social world of the receiver.

While the accuracy of information is important, we will concentrate here particularly upon the channels through which information flows—or should flow—for accelerated agricultural development. If the information does not reach the intended recipients, then, for their purposes, its quality is irrelevant. Yet as we diagnose the gaps and blockages in information flows, we are necessarily dealing with factors creating distortions in transmission and misunderstandings in reception and thus indirectly we are focusing upon some of the influences affecting the accuracy of information.

If we begin where new scientific information is generated in research institutes and universities, we tend to visualize a one-way flow beginning at these points and ending with the farmers. We need also to check on the flow in the reverse direction. Do farmers try to tell extension agents what they want and need? Do the agents respond? Do extension agents tell research people what kind of research projects and research reports would be especially useful to them? Do the researchers respond?

Reception of useful information is a necessary but not sufficient condition for improving farmer productivity. At the local level, we need to examine the ways in which the flow of information is coordinated with the flow of other resources poor farmers need. Similarly, for the organizations primarily concerned with the generation and transmission of information, those functions cannot be performed without the support of complementary human and physical resources, which must be supplied by the administration of the organizations involved in these stages of the information flow process.

Resources do not just spontaneously appear where men need them; they have to be provided through organizations. And where various types of resources need to be brought together at various points in a large program, the problems necessarily involve interorganizational relations. While recognizing that information is not everything, it will be useful to follow information flows as a vehicle for diagnosing the organizational and interorganizational problems.

In the following pages, we will be examining the information flow in the context of the following structural frameworks:

1. Organizational behavior and interorganization relations in agricultural research and extension.

2. The socioeconomic organization of agricultural activities.

3. Social structure and the distribution of power in rural areas.

4. Structural implications of social and technical innovations in rural areas.

Organizational Behavior and Interorganization Relations

In one country, within the agricultural research and development program for one of the principal crops, one unit is responsible for research and another unit is responsible for production of the new seed varieties developed out of the research program. While each unit is doing good work in its own particular field, their activities are highly interdependent, and a persistent conflict between the two unit heads has seriously impeded the progress of the program.

In discussing such problems with people in agricultural research and development, I encounter clichés rather than explanations. The most common of these are phrased in terms of the symbols *personality* and *bureaucracy*.

Conflict is explained in terms of personalities. People at the focal point of conflict do not have the kinds of personalities that permit them to get along together. While personalities play an important role in such conflicts, the personality explanation is of little use for practical purposes because administrators have very limited means of acting upon it. Adult personalities tend to be highly stable and resistant to change even under long periods of professional psychotherapy; therefore we must recognize that the boss of two men in conflict has little chance to change the personality of either of them. He might discharge or transfer one or both of them, hoping thus to come up with a combination of personalities that would be more compatible. However, the men in question may be performing well in every respect except in relation to each other; then it would be difficult to replace either of them with someone who might get along better and would perform equally well in other respects. Furthermore, there are certain to be social, political and bureaucratic precedents and pressures that limit the ability of any high level administrator to shuffle his people around until he comes up with a better combination of personalities.

The organization structure and pattern of work activities are often established in such a way that interpersonal conflict is almost inevitable. This suggests that we look beyond personalities in search of the organizational variables that tend to produce conflict or cooperation. In some cases we will find that changes in organization structure and work activities greatly reduce the debilitating effects of personality conflicts.

Once we go beyond personalities in our exploration, we find we have plunged into the study of bureaucracy (or organizational behavior), where we immediately encounter the second most popular cliché. Whatever problems of competition, incoordination, poor communication and duplication of activities we encounter, someone is bound to tell us, "That is bureaucracy for you!" The statement is offered as an explanation, yet in reality, of course, it only points to a problem. The words also have fatalistic implications: human nature being what it is, bureaucracies will always operate the way they do and there is nothing man can do about it except try his best to work despite the bureaucratic problems.

To rise above this fatalistic view, we must recognize that all bureaucracies are not alike. Different organizational models function in different ways and produce different results.

In both research and practice in the past it has been customary to see organizational problems in terms of authority or man-boss hierarchical relations. While the voluminous literature on managerial leadership will keep us from overlooking the importance of relations along this vertical dimension, we need to give special attention to previously neglected areas of concern: horizontal and diagonal relations. Horizontal relations are those between individuals at the same hierarchical level in different organizations or different units within the same organization. Diagonal relations are those between individuals at different hierarchical levels where the individual of superior status does *not* have authority over the person of inferior status.

For example, the conflict between the research and the seed production chiefs is a problem in horizontal relations. As I have indicated, even when the two men report to a common superior, it is very difficult to solve such a problem if we think and act exclusively in terms of authority. Where we are dealing with two men in horizontal or diagonal relation to each other but in different organizations, then clearly a failure of cooperation between them cannot be resolved by an appeal to authority. To deal effectively with such problems, we must learn to think and act in terms of strengthening horizontal and diagonal relations within and between organizations.

During the past decade, seven international research centers have been established: ILCA (livestock) in Ethiopia, CIP (potatoes) in Peru, CIAT (tropical agriculture) in Colombia, ICRISAT (semiarid tropical crops) in India, CIMMYT (corn and wheat) in Mexico, IITA (tropical agriculture) in Nigeria and IRRI (rice) in the Philippines. While the scientists in these centers may have some contacts directly with farmers in the course of their research, it is not the responsibility of an international center to get the information to farmers directly within any country. The ministries of agriculture in each country retain that responsibility. Nor is it the responsibility of an international center to substitute its own research program for that of each country. There are more than enough problems to go around, and international centers are expected to stimulate and strengthen the national programs. Furthermore, the new high-yielding seed varieties developed at any international center cannot be utilized in any given country until the national research and development program has tested the various strains under varying soil and climate conditions in its own country and in some cases has gone on to develop adaptations to local conditions.

Given this division of labor, an international center cannot meet its responsibilities without developing effective relations with national programs; even then, the benefits of research will not reach the farmers if there are breakdowns within the national program in the flow of information and complementary resources to the farmers.

The international center necessarily has a rather delicate relation with national agricultural programs. On the one hand, by bringing in some of the best experts in the world on some of the problems of concern to national agriculture, the center can greatly stimulate the work of its national colleagues. On the other hand, directors of the international centers are highly sensitive to the potential problems involved if they should appear to impose their views in such a way as to lead to conflicts or to excessive dependence on the part of the national program. Since the international center is better financed than the national program the national administrators may try to push off upon the international center activities that should be the responsibility of the national institutions, but how does one draw a line between national and international responsibilities so as to achieve the full potential of each field?

There is also a new set of relations between the international research center and the national universities of agriculture. Many critics have pointed out common weaknesses in the educational programs of agricultural universities in developing countries: excessive dependence upon reading and writing and inadequate opportunities for professors and students to undertake laboratory and field projects. Since the professionals of the international centers are particularly qualified by experience and interest to direct laboratory and field experiments, their participation in teaching programs in national universities can provide important contributions to those programs. Without abandoning their primary research responsibilities, scientists can only contribute a small fraction of the laboratory and field instruction needed by the national university in the host country of any center, but their participation in some teaching may help innovative university administrators to move their institutions out of the scholastic tradition toward more modern educational programs.

In some cases, scientists of an international center teach a course at a national university and, in general, arrangements are made for national and foreign students to do their thesis research under the guidance of staff members of the international center in collaboration with faculty members from the student's home university. However, these tend to be ad hoc arrangements worked out on the initiative of an individual scientist and with the at least passive acceptance of the center director who may see such collaboration simply as a means of gaining greater acceptance among fellow professionals in the host country. The full potential contribution of the international center to agricultural universities in the developing countries cannot be achieved unless the center makes such a contribution to institutional development one of its explicit policies, but to do so would involve a major change in emphasis and activities. It might be well for center scientists first to reflect upon the present pattern of their relations with universities and then to design small pilot projects in interorganizational collaboration in order to test out the possibilities and limitations of such a change in program and policies rather than plunging in with major commitments that might jeopardize the center's capacities to perform its primary research tasks.

Libraries are a key feature of any information processing system. They also provide a simple illustration of the potential and problems of interorganizational collaboration. Most of the publications needed for a good library in the agricultural sciences in a developing country must be imported, yet in most developing countries there are severe foreign exchange restrictions. Where a major agricultural university and a national agricultural research program have their facilities at the same location—as is the case in some developing countries—it is clearly to the economic advantage of both parties to pool their resources and, by eliminating duplication, extend their collection and build a higher quality library program. Where an international agriculture center is established at the same location—as has also happened—three-cornered arrangements could further increase the economic rewards of collaboration.

A library jointly supported and used by two or three organizations cannot be established by the authority of any one of them. It could only materialize through a series of discussions and negotiations among organizational administrators regarding the sharing of costs and benefits and through the mutually agreed upon design of a new organizational structure for the library. Most administrators are preoccupied with their own organizations and lack experience in interorganizational relations. Thus, while the potential gains of such collaboration are widely recognized, they are seldom realized in practice.

In agricultural research and development, horizontal and diagonal relations are complicated by the sorting out of professional personnel in organizational units in terms of their specialization. While it is convenient at times to speak of all these professionals as agricultural scientists, that label masks a great diversity among specialists in soil science, plant pathology, plant breeding, agricultural engineering and so on. Furthermore, there are specialists in particular crops, and one cannot assume that the expert in corn has more than a broad, general knowledge regarding rice cultivation. And finally social and behavioral scientists are increasingly seeking to join the ranks of agricultural scientists. Agricultural economists are by now reasonably accepted in this category, and some of the international centers are even venturing to reach out to include sociologists and anthropologists. I find the barriers to the disciplinary broadening of such programs not so much in the resistance of "hard" scientists as in their puzzlement as to how to use behavioral scientists effectively.

While interdisciplinary collaboration is favorably regarded, broadening the range of specialists expected to work together necessarily adds to the problems of communication among them, particularly in the case of the most recently included specialties, whose exponents need to learn new ways of thinking and speaking if they are to communicate effectively with their more established colleagues. Nor is this just a problem of learning to use a new set of verbal symbols. Different ways of conceptualizing the problems to be solved may lead to markedly different policy decisions. For example, suppose you are responsible for planning the agricultural development of an area of a developing nation. In recent years, the average yield of the principal crop has been one ton per hectare. Experts believe that, even with the seed varieties traditionally used in the area, productivity could be substantially increased. Two equally reputable research scientists seek your support for financing quite different research and development projects. Scientist A proposes a strategy designed to raise the average yield to two tons. Scientist B proposes a strategy with a potential yield of ten tons per hectare. If you can only back one project, where will you put your money?

The obvious answer seems to be, "Why settle for two when there is a chance of getting ten?"—unless you recognize that there is a catch to the question. The catch is that the two strategies are based upon radically different assumptions regarding the use of human and physical resources. The strategy of scientist B can produce something close to ten tons per hectare only if the farmer uses a large amount of fertilizer, improves his access to water, learns new methods of cultivation and increases the labor he puts into the farm. Instead of planning in terms of optimal conditions, scientist A decides to build his plan on the basis of existing conditions: infertile soil, little use of fertilizer, water only marginally adequate and farming methods that are changing only slowly. His aim is to develop a research program that will increase yields through making more efficient use of the inadequate plant nutrients in the soil and improving farming practice with minimal additional inputs.

If the assumptions of the two scientists are correct, then the potential yield of B's plan can be attained only by a small fraction of the farmers in the area: those who can finance heavy use of fertilizer, invest in improvements to their irrigation system, increase their use of labor and greatly improve their efficiency of farm management. Yet the doubling of yields predicted in A's plans might be achieved with only minor changes in the use of human and physical resources. If and when the farmer is able to add new inputs, he can further increase his yield. Such a strategy promises to meet the needs of the poor and small farmers.

While the opposing strategies are presented in terms of competition between two individuals, the differences may reflect the experience and ways of thinking characteristic of specialists in different disciplines. Agricultural economists and behavioral scientists tend to be unenthusiastic about the potential yields under optimal conditions and to concern themselves with the improvements obtainable under the realistic conditions that are likely to exist when the farmers try out the innovation. While the plant breeders do not assume that farmers will be able to equal the yields that scientists can obtain under carefully controlled experimental conditions, all their training and experience are likely to lead them toward the goal of the maximum possible yield for a given crop.

To be sure, this maximization goal has been pursued within certain constraints. Plant breeders have done important work in developing plant varieties that are disease resistant, drought resistant, adaptable to hot or cold climates, not sacrificing nutritional value for yield and so on. Yet little work has been done to develop plant varieties that can increase yields in infertile soil, since it is customarily assumed that adding the appropriate mix and amount of fertilizer can overcome this deficiency.

Rising prices and scarcity of fertilizer are likely to suggest to development planners and plant breeders that it would be a good idea to emphasize projects designed to produce seed varieties that would increase yields in low fertility soil, with little or no use of fertilizer. It is encouraging that some agronomists are currently giving more attention to the field testing of new plant varieties intended for making more efficient use of the plant nutrients in low fertility soil.

An analysis of the research and development system in agriculture must give major emphasis to the characteristic weaknesses in organizational and interorganizational relations of extension services, which are designed to provide the critical link between the producers of information and the ultimate consumers, the farmers. The deficiencies of extension are well documented in an impressive study of *Extension in the Andes*. From the end of World War II until 1970, the U.S. government placed its major agricultural development emphasis on the creation and financing of an extension system modeled after that of the United States. The support of this program for Latin America by the U.S. government was $30 million and the 12 host governments included in this study spent $55 million. This study, financed and published by AID, is especially noteworthy because it documents in great detail the failure of the organizational model and strategy that AID itself supported for so many years: "The lesson...of field investigations is clear: that sort of independent extension operation developed, not always intentionally, by the U.S. advisors and their counterparts is practically useless; extension only succeeds in improving productivity if it offers a profitable new technology in an economic regime that reduces risks, guarantees prices and/or offers credit." [10]

While the study found instances of local successes and successes with a particular crop, the researchers were unable to document any overall improvement in agricultural

productivity that could be attributed to the extension
model.

This costly failure can be partly explained in terms of
the exportation of an organizational model not well adapt-
ed to the conditions where it was applied, but it is important to note that the strategy was also based upon a
misreading of the history of agricultural development in
the United States. As is not generally recognized by non-
specialists, it was not until the 1930s that U.S. farmers
began to achieve significant increases in yields *per acre*.
Progress during previous decades was achieved primarily
through bringing more land under cultivation and through
mechanization which made possible spectacular increases
in production per man hour of labor.

These U.S.-style solutions of the pre-1930 period were
clearly inapplicable in developing countries. Governments
lacked the foreign exchange to finance large-scale
mechanization; furthermore, such a strategy would have
created enormous problems of displaced rural labor.
Where new land could be brought under cultivation, the
costs of promoting colonization projects were too high to
make this strategy practical on a nationwide basis.

In other words, in the 1940s the developing nations
needed help, especially in the kinds of research and development projects that were still in the early stages of development in the United States. We did not in fact have
the know-how we claimed to be exporting. Our scientists
had indeed made important advances in the development
of hybrid seed corn and in chemicals important for fertil-
ization and pest control, but the most important discover-
ies in the agricultural sciences require extensive field
testing in the areas where they are to be used before they
can be recommended to farmers with some confidence. En-
vironmental conditions of altitude, temperature, water
supply and nature of the soil vary so enormously from one
country to another or even from one area of a country to
another that the development of a new and more produc-
tive seed in an experimental laboratory provides no assurance that the seed will pay off when tried out by farmers.

At the time the extension program was launched, Latin American countries were in the early stages of developing their own agricultural research, and research findings from the United States could not be successfully applied without extensive field testing and further research and development to assure the fit of the innovation to local conditions. Since very little locally tested knowledge was available to extend to the farmers, agents had to import ideas from other countries, with dubious and unpredictable results. Even as agricultural research began to develop strength in Latin American countries, the extension services were so isolated from research as to inhibit a fruitful interchange, with extension agents taking to the field ideas developed by the national research groups and bringing back ideas about problems that researchers should be studying.

Even if the extension agents had more valuable knowledge to impart, E.B. Rice points out serious problems in getting this knowledge to the farmers. Experts in the field have recommended a ratio of one agricultural extension agent to every 500 families. Even though Rice concentrated on areas where extension success was considered better than average, and where presumably there was a higher ratio of extension agents than elsewhere, he found the prevailing ratios to be about one agent to every 10,000 families. This difference in numbers means that the frequency of agent contact with the farmers must necessarily be far lower than in the United States. To make even a superficial pass at covering his 10,000 farm families, the agent must move around rapidly, preventing him from gaining an understanding of local conditions and from developing the kind of rapport with individuals and groups upon which the transmission and application of knowledge depends. The effort to spread coverage to such unrealistic lengths also puts a premium on supplying agents with jeeps or other motorized vehicles, further adding to the expense of the operation.

The ratio problem also tends to push the agent toward concentrating his attention upon the larger farmers. Sup-

pose one of the areas in his territory contains one farmer
with 100 hectares and 100 farmers with one hectare each.
If the agent can persuade or help the 100-hectare man to
adopt an innovation designed to increase production, that
one intervention will have an impact over 100 hectares.
To have a similar impact on the other 100 hectares, the
agent would have to invest 100 times as many hours. Furthermore, even when he persuades the small farmers that
the proposed innovation is a good thing, he is likely to find
that they do not have the money to invest and cannot get
the credit they need, whereas the 100-hectare man either
has his own resources or has ready access to credit. In
this situation, knowing the way his performance is likely to
be evaluated by his superiors, the agent simply cannot af-
ford to spend much time on the 100 small farmers. Of
course, if he undertakes to get some of these 100 small
farmers together so that he works with a group rather
than with each one individually, the task of transmission of
information may become easier, but then he will have to
spend much of his time on stimulating group activity,
especially if no such activity has existed before. It is obviously much simpler for him to concentrate on the 100-
hectare man.

The deficiencies Rice found in the Andes are apparently
characteristic of extension services in many developing
nations. A recent book, based on research in 15 countries,
comes to the following conclusions:

> Throughout the developing world...they [extension ser-
> vices] are a poor match for the enormous tasks they will
> be called upon to perform in coming years....To a
> greater or lesser degree, most extension services:
> • go it alone, with insufficient cooperation with comple-
> mentary services;
> • operate haphazardly with neither priorities nor
> plans;
> • spread themselves too thinly to be effective;
> • concentrate their efforts on larger producers and
> major commercial crops while neglecting smaller farm-

ers and the local crops of key importance to subsistance
families;
- spend little effort diagnosing the differing needs of
their client farmers, and instead hand out standardized
recommendations that many of these clients find im-
practical and useless;
- depress the productivity of their field agents by neg-
lecting their inservice and refresher training, burden-
ing them with distracting chores, providing them with
inadequate transport, and failing to reinforce them with
mass media and other communication supports. [11]

The Socioeconomic Organization
of Agricultural Activities

To the urbanite, the farmer is simply someone who en-
gages in a lot of undifferentiated activities called farming.
But in the field, of course, we recognize that different
types of agricultural activities require drastically different patterns of work, division of labor and organization.
There is not only the obvious and important distinction between the raising of livestock and the raising of food
crops. We must also distinguish between raising of food
crops and raising products to be used in industrial activities, which may have quite different relations to the market. Even the category of raising of industrial raw materials may include products that have quite different
requirements in the management of farming activities. For
example, Milton Barnett [12] points out striking differences
in the patterns of work activity required for cultivation of
natural rubber and palm oil in Malaysia. He notes that a
rubber plantation can be operated with a looser system of
discipline and a less tightly coordinated set of activities
than is required for palm oil. If the rubber trees are not
tapped one day, they will wait for the next, and the liquid
tapped from the trees does not deteriorate so rapidly that
it must be rushed into processing. In contrast, there is
much less flexibility in the time period when palm nuts can
be harvested; once harvested, the nuts must be brought to

the processing plant within 24 hours or the crop will spoil. When we consider these differences, it is obvious that the same model for organization, management and leadership will not suit both sets of activities.

Where large numbers of farmers concentrate on raising a particular crop, the ability of development officials to help those farmers may well depend upon systematic socioeconomic studies focusing upon the activities involved in that type of farming. Consider the case of the potato in the Andean countries. The potato was first cultivated in the Andes, and it remains the most important food crop in very large areas of those countries. Since anthropologists have long been studying communities in which potatoes are grown, one would think we would have an adequate knowledge base regarding the socioeconomic activities involved in potato culture, yet this is far from the case. In these past studies, the potato has been simply incidental to the analysis of the kinship system, symbols and ceremonials, beliefs and practices.

To begin to fill this knowledge gap, students of anthropology, under the direction of Jorge Flores of the University of Cuzco, have carried out a field study of a peasant community, extending the more traditional anthropological interests to provide systematic knowledge regarding the beliefs and agricultural practices of the farmers. The students are examining the practices of planting, cultivating and harvesting the potato, studying the consumption of potatoes in the community, observing the ways in which potatoes are stored and noting the ways in which potatoes are bartered for other products or are sold directly or through intermediaries. In other words, the project is designed to provide a systematic account of the technical, economic, cultural and social aspects of potatoes for the community. No immediate application of this research knowledge is planned. The rationale for the project is that, until we have this kind of integrated knowledge regarding potatoes in peasant life, we will not have a solid foundation upon which to build improvements in agricultural development in communities depending heavily upon potatoes.

A recent experience on an International Rice Research Institute project illustrates the interrelation of social and technical factors in water management. [13] The researchers found in one small area in the Philippines a ratio of almost four to one in comparing the highest and lowest rice yields. They further found that a major part of this differential could be explained in terms of adequacy or inadequacy of the supply of irrigation water. The farmers located close to the head of the lateral had more water than they needed, whereas those toward the opposite end had much less than they needed.

The technical problem was straightforward: to make the changes that would redistribute water so that no farms would have a surplus of water and none would have inadequate water. As a first step in carrying out this plan, four technicians began setting up equipment to measure the flow of water at different points in the system.

The project was brought to an abrupt halt when the technicians were arrested and put in jail. The farmers toward the head of the lateral objected, not because they misunderstood the purposes of the project, but because they recognized that the redistribution of water could leave them short in an especially dry year. Furthermore, the new system would add greatly to their work in water management on their own farms. When they almost always had a surplus, they needed to give little attention to the management of their part of the irrigation system. Under the new program, they might hope to have adequate water at all times but only through giving careful and continued attention to the management of the water that flowed through their property. As might be expected, the farmers who were in the advantageous position in the irrigation system had more political power than those at the other end of the lateral. In fact, one of the farmers at the head of the lateral was the son of the mayor, and it was he who had the technicians arrested. While the IRRI project people, through appealing to officials in the national irrigation authority, were later able to work out arrangements to proceed with the plan, the strong opposition they encountered at the outset from the more favored farmers illustrates the importance of combining social with technical planning of interventions.

Since realizing the full potential of the new seed varieties and methods of cultivation requires irrigation water in many regions, it is clear that improving the effectiveness of water distribution systems is of the utmost importance. Improvement programs must be based upon a combination of social and technical planning. For such projects to be effective, planners require a much better interdisciplinary knowledge base than is currently available to them. Previous studies indicate that the same technology and technical methods of water control can be used in different countries or in different areas of the same country under quite different sociopolitical management systems. If the development planner seeks to intervene to improve the technical functioning of a given irrigation system, without understanding the sociopolitical organization of that system, he is bound to fall short of his technical objectives. A research team made up of agricultural engineer Gilbert Levine, economist L. F. Small, anthropologist Milton Barnett and sociologist E. W. Coward is currently engaged in comparative studies along this line in several countries in Southeast Asia.

Social Structure and the Distribution of Power

The social organization of agricultural activities in rural areas inevitably shapes—and is shaped by—the social structure and the distribution of power; therefore, it is impossible to separate the two topics completely. For example, in examining the social organization of an irrigation system, we necessarily become involved with problems of power. My purpose at this point is to put in more systematic and explicit form some aspects of power and social structure that need to be considered by development planners.

In areas primarily devoted to agriculture, the distribution of power is intimately related to the system of land tenure. This means not only the equality/inequality in amount of land owned but also includes differences in quality of land and in access to water. Generally, it is safe to assume that those who own more and better land and have better access to water will enjoy higher social status, have greater wealth and possess more political power. The greater the inequality in the distribution of these resources, the greater is likely to be the disparity in political power between the top and the bottom of the social structure.

The land tenure system also includes tenancy arrangements, from direct rental payments to various forms of sharecropping. The value of a given arrangement to the parties involved is unknown unless we have information on the amount of rent paid in relation to the value of the crops grown or the distribution of costs and benefits involved in the sharecropping contract. Furthermore, we cannot assume that the value to the parties will remain constant over time. If the landlord finds it more profitable to mechanize and operate all his land directly, he is likely to try to reduce or eliminate tenants and sharecroppers.

At or near the bottom of the social pyramid are the part-time and full-time laborers. The part-timers are generally small farmers who are not fully occupied on their own land and cannot support their families without hiring themselves out to the larger farmers. The full-timers are generally landless laborers, fully dependent upon their wages.

On the traditional haciendas of the Andean countries, those at the bottom, known as *colonos*, have occupied a status similar to that of serfs on the medieval European manor. They owned no land but had a right to cultivate a small plot in the most disadvantageous part of the hacienda in return for approximately three days a week of labor service to the landlord. In addition, they received a trifling cash payment, plus perhaps some coca to chew.

Where the land tenure system is marked by a high degree of inequality, those toward the bottom of the pyramid always far outnumber those at the top, so one might assume that some degree of power equalization could be achieved if the lower-class people would organize themselves to confront the local elite. In fact, this has happened in some parts of the world. In Peru, we have examined peasant movements whereby *colonos* have not only gotten themselves organized but also, after a struggle, have managed to push out the landlords and take over the land themselves.

This possibility of organization and successful confrontation appears much more likely for *colonos* and full-time laborers than for renters and sharecroppers, who are likely to be insecure enough in their relations with the landlords to hold back from any solidarity movement. Especially where part-time labor is in abundant supply, the small holders who supplement their incomes in working for the large owners are likely also to avoid confrontation. While these general conclusions may appear obvious, their implications are rarely taken into account by writers and planners in community and agricultural development. Let us illustrate how differences in social structure and the distribution of power should affect the plans of development people.

Assume that the change agent aims to improve the lot of lower-class rural people and hopes to help them set up some kind of cooperative organization. A cooperative is likely to be prescribed to meet almost any kind of problem on the countryside because the vision of people working together to help themselves gladdens the heart of any change agent, and also because it is obviously more efficient for an agent to work with and through the leaders of an organization rather than work with each family separately.

The change agent must cope with two basic structural problems before launching his project. The first involves the social organization of agriculture. More rural cooperatives fail than succeed, and the differences between failure and success do not depend so much upon fidelity to Rochdale principles as upon the appropriateness of the organizational form to the activities it is supposed to support. For example, it seems to be more difficult to build a successful producers' cooperative (in which the members jointly produce the output) than a marketing cooperative (in which the members market through the organization the produce of each member). Furthermore, among marketing cooperatives it seems more difficult to build an organization to sell a variety of crops in various markets than it is to build a single crop organization—especially when that crop goes largely into the export market and commands an attractive price.

It is important to note that the above tentative generalizations are based upon personal impressions, conversations with colleagues and interpretations of organization theory. Strange as it may seem, in view of the enormous popularity of the cooperative idea, little research has yet been done upon the structural elements making for success or failure. Missionaries of the cooperative movement seem to assume that a cooperative is a cooperative and that the main requirements for success are dedication to cooperative principles and skillful leadership.

The second structural condition is provided by the social structure and distribution of power in the area where the change agent plans to intervene. The situation that seems to be most open to organization building is one where there are large numbers of small farmers concentrated in the same area, with few or no large landowners. There the change agent may expect to find widely shared problems and interests and little internal opposition.

Where the pattern of ownership is more unequal and especially where there are a number of very large landowners, the change agent dedicated to helping the small farmers is likely to have more difficulty in finding the broadly shared common interests and common perceptions of problems upon which to build an organization. Furthermore, the change agent should expect opposition from the large landowners who suspect that his intervention may threaten their interests. Not only differences in size of holdings but also the degree of dependence of the small upon the large and vice versa are involved. If the

large landowners have self-contained units, not relying
upon small holders for supplementary labor or for sharecropping arrangements, organization of the small holders
will seem less threatening to the large ones and thus less
likely to provoke their opposition. If a project to organize
the small holders leads them to withdraw from the labor
market in order to devote all their time to their own farms
and related activities, the large owners will face shortages of labor and rising wages. The change agent will
probably find it impossible to organize tenants and share-
croppers unless a broad peasant movement is in progress
so the dependent farmers come to believe that the power
of the large landlords is beginning to disintegrate.

While serfs and full-time laborers are likely to be more
receptive to organization, clearly the traditional community development approach will not work with them. They
are under the domination of the landlord, and any official
approach to them must be made through him. Can we
imagine a community developer knocking on the door of
the hacendado and asking, "Don Fulano, is it all right
with you if I try to organize your *colonos*?" When *colonos*
and laborers are organized, the job is done not by change
agents working for government or a private development
agency but by organizers for a union or a peasant movement.

Aside from revolution, there is, of course, one alterna-
tive to organization from the bottom in situations of great
socioeconomic equality: a land reform program in which
the power is mobilized at the national level to overpower
the elites in rural areas. Land reform is a problem of such
scope and complexity that it cannot be dealt with here except in passing. However, it is important for the change
agent to be able to diagnose local conditions so as to avoid
wasting time and energy upon a personal intervention
where there is no possibility of improving the lot of people
at the bottom unless land reform is first carried out.

Structural Implications of Social
and Technological Innovations in Rural Areas

Behavioral scientists have been so obsessed with "resistance to change," which is presumed to be embedded in human nature, that they have failed to consider the structural aspects of change. The implicit assumption has been that a change is a change is a change and that therefore the problem for the change agent is to develop a social process that will overcome "resistance to change." While the manner of introducing the change has an influence on its acceptance, the type of change may well be even more important.

As has been argued elsewhere, [14] different types of innovations may have radically different consequences in the distribution of costs and benefits and therefore may require quite different social strategies for their introduction. We have suggested the following typology:

1. *Individual direct.* Here the individual farmer bears all of the costs and gains all of the benefits. Such would be the case on the family farm where the family tries a new seed, invests in fertilizer, insecticide and so on, providing that these changes do not involve any changes in the communal system of water control. While it may be advantageous to the change agent to work through the local power structure to get large numbers of people interested in the innovation, the individual farmer can make his decision without regard to the decisions of others.

2. *Individual through group, with equitable sharing of costs and benefits.* Such would be the case with community-wide projects: a reservior to provide potable water, a road improvement to provide better access to the market and so on. For such projects, the mobilization of all community households is expected, but people can be appealed to in terms of the equities of sharing in costs and benefits. Yet there can be differences in the ease or difficulty of achieving equity. For example, the family that declines to contribute labor to the building of the reservoir

can be required to pay a fine before connecting its home to the system, whereas it is hardly feasible to prevent a non-participating family from sharing in the benefits of the road improvement.

3. *Unequal distribution of costs and benefits.* Regardless of the skill of change agents or political leaders, the very nature of the project promises to benefit some people at the expense of others. For example, a government financed reforestation project pays community members who plant the trees, but the project reduces the communal grazing area, thus having adverse effects particularly upon a few families with large numbers of animals.

4. *Controlling individual interests in favor of group interests.* If the community as a whole is to benefit, individual members must be restrained from doing what otherwise would be rewarding to them and their families. Such cases are often found in the field of animal husbandry. If the community faces a problem of overgrazing, and if steps are not taken to limit or reduce the size of the herd, the pasturage will be destroyed, with disastrous consequences for everyone. However, if every other family sticks to the rules and one family gets some extra animals on the range, that family stands to reap extra benefits. Similarly, in the case of sheep herding, if every family in the community or cooperative sells or castrates its low-grade male animals, the members can increase total profits by purchasing better animals or by other methods. But the goal of each member is to increase his own herd size. (This also involves type 3, since members with larger herds will have more inferior animals to sacrifice for the common good.)

It should be evident that these four types of projects present quite different problems of organization and control. While the second is more complex than the first, the first two might lend themselves well to a traditional community development strategy, with the emphasis upon participation and group discussion. The third type of change brings us inevitably to face problems affecting the distribution of political power within and beyond the community. The fourth type hardly lends itself to implementation through a voluntary cooperative approach and must therefore require some outside political leverage. This suggests the importance of examining the social distribution of costs and benefits in different types of innovations before making much headway in devising improved intervention strategies.

The structural implications of change projects cannot be considered apart from the social structure and distribution of power. In a farming area that is relatively homogeneous in size of holdings and type of activities, a change agent will find it much easier to develop a type 2 project (individual through group, with equitable sharing of costs and benefits) than in an area with large differences in these respects. In an area where the distribution of land is highly unequal, many projects designed to improve the lot of the small farmers will involve unacceptable costs and/or inadequate benefits to the large farmers.

This conclusion suggests that theorists of community development need to stop giving exclusive attention to social processes of personal involvement, participation and cooperation in order to learn more about the organization and management of social conflict.

4

Strategies for Research and Development in Agriculture

The previous discussion leads us to some useful conclusions for both research and practice. For research, I shall concentrate particularly on the potential contributions of the behavioral scientists, but this also involves how our studies may be integrated with research in other disciplines. If you misdiagnose a problem, you are unlikely to solve that problem. Therefore, the first requirement for behavioral scientists is to abandon the misdiagnoses of the past.

This means junking the myth of the passive peasant. It does not mean going to the opposite extreme, assuming that peasants are endowed with infallible folk wisdom, ready to seize upon any promising opportunity presented them. We simply should assume that, in general, the small farmer is far from satisfied with his situation and is quite prepared to accept changes—even drastic changes—when he perceives them to be to his advantage. This assumption shifts the focus of research from the character and personality of the farmer to the socioeconomic conditions that lead him to accept or reject changes. It also leads us away from the sterile assumption that change of any sort tends to provoke resistance and leads us to describe and classify the various types of changes that may be offered to the farmer so as to understand why he may be receptive to one type and reject another.

We must also abandon our studies of the diffusion of innovation, insofar as those studies are based upon tracing the acceptance of *the* innovation. It is now painfully evident that the only ones capable of making effective use of a particular innovation in agriculture are those who are able to combine it with other resources already in their command or made available to them as a package. By this logic, the problem of bringing the benefits of innovation to the small farmer involves developing means of providing him with the package of resources he needs.

It is just as important that planners of agricultural development abandon the myth of the passive peasant. Such a reorientation of the power elite will not come easily. The effects of social structure and culture may persist even after the traditional elite has been replaced by a government dedicated to an ideology of popular participation in changes designed to benefit low-income people. For example, consider the following statement of one of the foremost shapers of the ideology and practices of the present Peruvian regime.

> We must work in this direction, to make the people understand that we are not going to achieve in a day the changes we hope for. We must recognize with sufficient clarity the cultural level of the worker in the lowest stratum of our society. For this reason I call this society ignorant, and therefore the greatest obstacle that the revolution faces is ignorance, because the clear needs of society cannot be understood by our people and they are not to blame for not having had the opportunity to educate themselves. [15]

According to this doctrine, the ignorance of the peasant, the Indian and the industrial worker are no longer considered inherent. These lower-class people cannot be blamed for their ignorance; they have had no opportunity to educate themselves. Without education men remain ignorant, and it is up to those individuals who have obtained the knowledge to educate and indoctrinate their less fortunate fellow citizens.

The fallacy of this orientation lies in its failure to understand the interrelations of intelligence, experience, formal education and knowledge. The implicit assumption is that ignorance is transformed into knowledge solely by education. Without denying the importance of improved education for rural people, we must emphasize that knowledge arises out of experience as well as out of a formal educational program. (Of course, the ideal road to knowledge is one that combines experience with formal education.) Confusing knowledge with formal education, the professional assumes the small farmer has learned nothing useful in 20 to 40 years of farming and fails to recognize the importance of his own lack of experience in the field, where the small farmer has been living all his life.

The greatest obstacle facing agricultural development is not the ignorance of the peasants but rather the conviction of so many agricultural professionals that the peasants are ignorant and thus incapable of contributing intellectually to the progress of their communities and their country. Perhaps the behavioral scientist may play a useful role in helping professionals and small farmers develop a dialogue in harmony with the objectives of rural development.

The required reorientation of attitudes toward small farmers has implications both for research and practice. If we reject the passive peasant assumption, then we assume that small farmers will actively seek ways to improve their lot and that, while many such efforts will be frustrated, we will find (as we ourselves have found) developing communities that have been very largely self-propelled.

My purpose in proposing studies of such self-propelled communities is not to claim small farmers would be better off if outsiders left them alone. I am simply proposing that social and historical studies of successful cases of indigenous development will provide planners with basic information needed in order to develop more effective intervention plans. If you know which way the ball is rolling and with what speed, you have a much better chance of intervening to accelerate the ball along the current pathway or to modify its direction than would be the case if you mistakenly assume that the ball is standing still and that you must overcome its inertia and also provide its direction. The need here is not for more studies of the "typical" peasant community but rather for the discovery and systematic study of those cases which have broken out of the pattern of economic stagnation that is so widespread.

This reorientation of views also suggests the urgent need for the organizational system to become more responsive to initiatives from the farmers. If we finally assume that peasants have learned something from their years of experience, then the system must encourage feedback of suggestions, criticisms and demands from the farmers. It is not enough to feed good information to the farmers; any development system is defective unless it provides for feedback from the farmers.

An Organizational Framework for Research and Action

For behavioral scientists I am proposing a shift of emphasis from studies of the attitudes and beliefs of small farmers toward an organizational framework in which any organization studied is seen in the context of the total organizational system of agricultural development. This means not only giving attention to the vertical relations within each organization but also, and most particularly, examining the horizontal and diagonal relations that link (or should link) the various units that make up the total organizational system.

Even before new research is done, the adoption of an organizational framework will enable the development planner to arrive at more useful diagnoses of problems. He will then recognize that it is futile to strive simply to build a better extension service, a better research organization and a better agricultural university when those organizations are each seen in isolation. A good extension service does not exist without effective linkages to an agricultural research organization. A research organization may be well rated by tradition-minded agricultural scientists, nationally and internationally, if its scientists do "interesting work" and publish frequently in the best professional journals, but the farmers don't read the technical papers and, unless the research program is effectively linked with some human service to bring the fruits of new knowledge to the farmers, and to bring the concerns of the farmers to the researchers, the organization's research output will only enhance the professional standing of its scientists.

It is hard to imagine a good university teaching and research program in agriculture that is entirely isolated from contact with national and international research programs and that lacks the kinds of field work programs that bring professors and students into frequent contact with extension agents and farmers.

Making this organizational framework explicit should help planners recognize that agricultural development is not simply the sum of the outputs of each separate organization involved. Unless these organizations are effectively linked together, little of their outputs ever gets to the farmers. The first step in planning should therefore be to visualize the total agricultural development organizational system. If the planner then seeks to diagnose the most critical weaknesses in the system, he is likely to find that he must devote his attention particularly to the long-neglected problem of interorganizational linkages.

Experimenting with New Organizational Models

Research has progressed enough to diagnose the common deficiencies in the organizational systems for agricultural development but not far enough to prescribe in detail the types of organizational models required to eliminate these deficiencies. Agricultural scientists are accustomed to doing experiments in plant breeding and other aspects of crop production. They should now extend this creativity into experimentation with new organizational models. Behavioral scientists can help in the designing of models worth testing and especially in developing the research methods required to determine whether the new model performs better than the old.

Organizational experimentation needs to be done especially in two spheres: building new horizontal relations at the top and middle levels of the organizations involved in the flow of information from research to delivery of services to the farmers and, in local areas, building new organizational forms for supplying and coordinating the resources small farmers need.

For the first sphere, the establishment of some sort of interorganizational committee naturally comes to mind, but such a committee will exist only on paper unless it has some resources at its command, can provide incentives to stimulate interunit collaboration and can gather information to diagnose problems and determine whether in fact improved collaboration is developing.

Top- and middle-level collaboration among organizations is necessary but not sufficient to solve the problem of combining and integrating the wide variety of resources needed by the small farmer at the local level. The problem of extension is not only its inadequate linkage with research but also, as Coombs points out, "Many agricultural extension services operate without organic links or close collaboration with credit, input and marketing services handled by other organizations." [16]

In his evaluation of 25 rural adult education programs in 15 developing countries, Coombs gives the highest marks to those in which "extension services are fully meshed with virtually all complementary services for agricultural development." He cites as examples CADU (Ethiopia), Comilla (now Bangladesh), PACCA (Afghanistan) and Puebla (Mexico), but even in these cases his brief descriptions make it clear that these new models, while representing important advances over past practice, have faced serious problems of their own. Therefore, we should look to these cases not as final solutions but rather as models whose structures and functioning require further study in order to aid us in designing better models for the integration of resources at the farmer level. If a very small fraction of the money invested in crop research were directed toward this organizational problem, we might expect an important research breakthrough in the near future.

Up to this point, the needs for change have been considered in terms of the implicit assumption that it is up to the development planners and administrators to so restructure the total organizational system that the employees within the system are able to and motivated to serve the small farmers better. In other words, even though my aim is to help the people at the bottom, I have been assuming that the pressures for change will come from the top down. Suppose instead we think of a system where the pressures for services to farmers flow from the bottom up. The Farmers' Associations of Taiwan [17] represent such a model.

An adequate description and evaluation of the Farmers' Associations is beyond the scope of this book. For present purposes, it is important only to note that, while the Associations have been strongly shaped by laws and administrative regulations, they nevertheless do represent a novel model in which resources and services are under the control of the Association, with the extension agent being its employee. This type of structural arrangement is likely to make the agent more responsive to the ideas and needs of the farmers than is the case where the agent's rewards and penalties are under the control of his superiors in the bureaucracy.

We have been considering deficiencies in the knowledge of extension agents and deficiencies in the relations between extension and research and extension and the complementary resources needed by farmers. We have touched on the ratio problem noting that the study of *Ex-*

tension in the Andes found a ratio of one agent to 10,000 farm families, compared to a ratio of one to 500 recommended by experts. Does this suggest that the Andean countries would have achieved better results if they had had 20 times as many agents in the field? Quite apart from our own conclusions on the deficiencies of extension, given the fact that the one to 10,000 ratio produced no results that could be measured in production, it would have been folly for the governments to shoulder the enormous financial burdens required to substantially reduce that ratio. Furthermore, Coombs cites figures for 19 countries with ratios running from one to less than 500 to over 15,000, and he ventures no conclusions that would relate the effectiveness of extension to these differences in ratios. [18]

The problem of extension is not only the number of farmers and the geographical distance to cover but also the social distance gap. In many parts of the United States, the extension agent is dealing with a clientele not much different from himself in education and social status. In a developing nation, however, the status gap between the agent and the small farmer is far greater. Where a rigid pattern of social stratification has existed, as is true in many developing nations, the agent may find it difficult to believe that the farmer with little or no formal education and an income perhaps only one-twentieth of his own might have any knowledge and ideas worth considering.

Rather than spending more money to reduce the number of farm families to be reached by each agent and to select and train agents with the social skill and the will to bridge the status gap, planners might experiment with inserting a linking role between agents and small farmers. In the Comilla project "the village people chose one of their own number to serve as their educational liaison with outside sources of knowledge relevant to their needs (as *they* saw their needs)." [19] These representatives received special training and were expected to take the initiative in seeking assistance to meet the needs of the villagers and also to consult and work with project staff in the introduction of new ideas proposed by the professionals.

While the basic idea is simple, development planners will need to do a good deal of social experimentation before they can determine, for their own country and for different areas of that country, how the liaison representatives should be chosen, what incentives (material and nonmaterial) they should receive, how much and what kind of training they need, how extension and other services for farmers need to be reorganized so as to provide the support needed for the new role and so on.

A Strategy for Field Experiments
in Agricultural Production

While I have stressed the importance of taking an experimental approach to the discovery and development of better organizational models, we should recognize that most field experiments in agricultural development will continue to be directed toward the increase in crop yields at the farm site. A social process framework for such experiments might improve their effectiveness.

Before presenting a strategy for field experiments, let us review the factors involved in the earlier discribed failures of change agents.

Lack of interdisciplinary coordination. We cannot assume that the agricultural scientists are producing knowledge ready to be extended to the farmers by the extension agent. A good deal of work needs to be done in integrating knowledge and ideas of various disciplines and balancing biological, engineering, social, economic and political considerations before we can be confident that we have knowledge useful to the farmer.

Skipping of steps in research and development. Past failures have arisen out of efforts to apply knowledge and use seeds developed in the national or international research laboratory in an area where conditions of soil and climate are different. This is now a well-recognized problem; the necessity of field testing an innovation before it is used in a given area is generally accepted. Nevertheless, it is still likely that national planners will feel under such pressure for results as to short cut this local testing and adaptation process, thus increasing risks and losses to farmers.

Unrealistically large program interventions. Given the urgency of the food production and farm income problems, politicians are inclined to pick up any plausible new idea and seek to mount a program to put that idea to use on a nationwide basis or at least in some large region. Perhaps the most spectacular example of this tendency is what came to be known as the Bimas case[20] in Indonesia. In order to attain self-sufficiency in rice, government decision-makers in 1968 established a goal of increasing production somewhat more than 50 percent within a five-year period. Recognizing that such an ambitious objective was beyond the capacity of the government, the planners decided to by-pass their own agricultural bureaucracy by channeling the flow of new and increased inputs through commercial organizations. Still, the agricultural bureaucracy could not be left out altogether, since regional administrators were needed to set regional production targets and report on results. After less than two years of confusion and conflict among government agencies and private firms involved in Bimas, the whole program collapsed. As Hansen notes, "The size of the target overwhelmed the existing structures of administration and substantially reduced the effectiveness of the entire campaign to achieve self-sufficiency."

Failure to involve small farmers in planning and evaluation of the results of innovations. This is a natural consequence of widespread belief in the myth of the passive peasant.

To discover needed improvements in the research and development of increasing yields, it may be helpful to examine this process in industry. In a major company with a well-established research program, the process involves a flow of activities and information through a number of organizational units, beginning with basic research and ending with production. In industry, basic research involves studying the physical and chemical properties of the materials in common use by the company, without any immediate applied purpose, although of course it is assumed that increasing basic knowledge will lead eventually to application. Applied research begins at a point where management and the scientists can visualize an eventual product, and the scientists move on to carry out the studies necessary to solve the scientific and engineering problems that will be encountered in production. The next step is to launch pilot production in a department or plant assigned to that purpose. Here the firm is producing what it hopes will resemble the final product but only on a small scale, where product and production process can be further studied and modified as problems arise. This involves industrial engineering to determine the number and nature of jobs needed for production, how the work flow should be organized among the workers, what rates of pay will be called for and, finally, what the per unit cost of the product is likely to be when the firm moves on to mass production.

Whether the project moves from pilot production to mass production depends not only on findings of cost and engineering studies but also upon market research and market testing. Here the researchers try to find out what potential customers expect and want in this type of product. If the product is bound to be expensive in production and sales price, extensive market testing may be required in order to provide some assurance that causes for customer complaints are eliminated in advance. For testing, the pilot product may be placed in a number of homes, with the customer being offered a reduced price on the test model and attractive terms for eventual substitution of the final commercial model in return for being interviewed periodically by company personnel over a period of months or even years regarding the good and bad points of the test model.

This examination suggests two major differences from agriculture in the organization of research and development in industry: the greater length of the chain of activities and organizational units involved in the process and the much more active involvement of the final users of the product. When the agricultural research process reaches the small farmer, all too often the expert seems to tell him: "We know what is good for you. This is what you ought to do." In industry the market research and testing people are not trying to tell the customer what is good for him and what he ought to want. They are trying to learn from the customer what he thinks is wrong with the product in the hope that such information will enable management to make improvements that will increase customer satisfaction and acceptance. An analysis of past failures and comparison with industrial research and development suggests a strategy for innovation in agriculture along the following lines:

1. *Start small.* A pilot operation can be closely studied so that adjustments can be made before major problems arise and so that those in charge of the field experiment have an intimate knowledge of what is going on.

A small-scale beginning makes it easier to bring together the package of resources small farmers will need if the experiment is to be successful. As the introduction of the innovation is planned, the planners should also work out methods of gathering information to document the process of innovation, noting the difficulties encountered as well as the gains achieved. A small beginning also greatly reduces the resources in personnel and motor vehicles required. The program does not make major commitments of such resources until a small-scale effort has indicated sufficient promise to make it worth applying on a somewhat larger scale.

The admonition to start small does not mean that only one experiment should be undertaken at one time. A research and development system may have the capacity to carry out several small field experiments at the same time. As results come in, the planners can then determine which experiments should be abandoned and which tried out further on a larger scale.

2. *Involve the small farmers actively in the develop-*

ment of the experiment. This principle should be applied
even in the first step of deciding where the field experiment shall be located. Instead of approaching a group of
farmers as if to let them know that they are the lucky people who have been selected to receive the benefits of the innovation, the planners should select a small number of
communities where conditions of soil, climate and land
tenure are appropriate for the experiment. Instead of
going around from place to place to try to sell participation in the experiment to each group of farmers, the planners should pursue a more exploratory and participatory
strategy. From village to village, they should conduct a
series of discussions along the following lines: explain to
the farmers the nature of the innovation; say that they
believe participation in the experiment will bring benefits
to the farmers and yet caution that they cannot guarantee
results, adding that there is necessarily some element of
risk involved. They then should proceed to explore with
the villagers what the project might be able to offer and
what the farmers might be able to offer to the project. For
example, the project might offer credit for the purchase of
the new package (seeds, fertilizer, insecticides and so on).
The project might also offer some form of crop insurance
so as to cushion the farmers against possible losses in
case the innovation does not work out well. Some kind of
assistance in marketing the crop might be arranged. The
project might also offer special training to several
members of the community and also briefer instructional
sessions for anyone interested. The parties could then discuss how the instructional sessions should be organized,
how the potential paraprofessionals should be selected
and trained and so on.

What can the villagers offer the project? Village leaders can assume responsibilities in explaining the project
to their fellows and answering questions about it. The
villagers also may be able to offer food and lodging to project personnel while they are in the community, thus making a solid financial contribution to the project. The most
important contribution the villagers can make is informa-

tion. The project people should emphasize the importance of accurate and detailed information on agricultural practices as well as on the results of these practices. Where enough people in the community have a level of literacy to permit it, farmers participating in the program can offer to fill out records documenting their practices—presumably with the advice and assistance of project personnel. Where this level of literacy is not found, the parties can discuss the most practical methods for the small farmers to give project people the information needed, thus documenting the total course of the experiment. Finally, the small farmers participating in the experiment can offer to—or be asked to—participate fully in the evaluation of the experiment after all the results have been gathered.

3. *Expand in easy stages.* One of the great hazards facing this strategy is that, if a small-scale intervention in agriculture appears to be successful, government officials will exert great pressure to have the ideas immediately put into practice on a national or at least on a large regional scale. The hazards of this jump from a regional to a national program are well illustrated in James Green's classic article on "Success and Failure in Technical Assistance." There the author describes how a new type of training program for agricultural extension personnel in Pakistan appeared to be such a success at one training institute that the government insisted in expanding the program at once to a nationwide basis. The result was that the project planners and organizers left the original institute before the innovation had been institutionalized and, when they had finished starting the activities all over the country, returned to find no trace of the original innovation in the continuing programs of the institute where they began—nor was there later any evidence of success for the program on a nationwide basis.

Project planners need to recognize that every significant increase in the scale of their program introduces a new set of problems into their own organizational activities and into the management of the flow of resources to the farmers. If the beginning is made in one community or several small communities, the project planners can be personally involved with the farmers and thus be in a position to recognize quickly any problems arising between project personnel and the farmers. As the program moves to a stage where such direct contacts are no longer possible, planners face new problems in planning and developig a new organization structure, training the people to carry out the activities they themselves performed in the first stage and establishing a communications network for the gathering of information necessary for the evaluation of the program.

When a program begins in one small area, it is relatively easy to supply the credit, fertilizer, pesticides, technical assistance and other elements of the total package necessary for success. The government would have little problem arranging for this preferential access in the small experimental area because the preferences shown this area will have a minimal effect upon the resources available elsewhere. As the program moves on to successively larger stages, the problems of providing resources in program areas become increasingly difficult because the resources called for represent increasingly larger drains on supplies needed in other parts of the country. Furthermore, a technically successful program, if expanded too rapidly, can cause a drop in market prices with severe losses to both participating and nonparticipating farmers. Planners need not only to adjust the stages of expansion to the availability of the necessary inputs but also to change the ways these inputs have been traditionally supplied to farmers.

When the program is operating in the first small experimental area, the planners can work out special arrangements with the agricultural bank and the suppliers of the other necessary inputs to make the package readily available in that area. The special arrangements for a community or a set of small communities cannot simply be multiplied as the program expands. The planners face a set of entrenched institutions with established patterns of activities. These patterns can be changed, but they certainly will not adjust automatically in response to increasing demands for inputs by the expanding research and development program. Unless these organizational changes of the supplying of inputs can be carried out on a large scale, the program planners will find that what they are doing on a large scale bears little resemblance to what they were able to do on a small scale.

These general recommendations may have more meaning if viewed in relation to an actual project, which, while still in its early stages of development, appears to embody a number of features I have in mind. The Huasahuasi project is an interdisciplinary research and development effort in a peasant community. Huasahuasi is a strategic point for intervention in Peru, since this highland community has 30,000 hectares in potatoes and produces a large percentage of the seed potatoes used on the coast. Another important factor in the selection of this community was the personal history of the project leader, Ulises Moreno, who was born and brought up in Huasahuasi and comes from a family associated with potato farming. Moreno is probably the first Peruvian—and perhaps the first man from any country—who returned to his peasant community to give a public report on his doctoral thesis. Having finished the defense of his thesis in plant physiology before his Cornell professors, Moreno went to great pains not only to translate the ideas and information into Spanish but also to learn to talk about the technical and scientific aspects of cultivation of potatoes in language readily understandable to the common people of Huasahuasi. The public meeting for the thesis report was held in the evening in the central plaza. Moreno illustrated his talk with projection on the wall of the church of slides made from the potatoes that he had taken with him from Huasahuasi to Cornell for analysis and experimentation. The members of the community could thus see on a large scale some of the problems of plant disease and pests with which they were struggling in their regular round of farm activities.

The return of the native son stimulated the leaders of

the community to ask Ulises Moreno, who had resumed his position as professor at the Agrarian University, to organize a project to provide assistance to the potato growers of Huasahuasi. Moreno was able to raise modest financial support from the university and from the Ministry of Agriculture within the terms of a ministerial resolution authorizing the university to send professors and students out to offer technical assistance to communities and cooperatives. He then went about organizing an interdisciplinary team of seven professors, including himself, representing specialties in plant physiology, soils and fertilizers, disease control, pest control, economics, sociology and agricultural extension. The professors selected ten students from a list of candidates drawn from the programs in agronomy, economics and planning, biological sciences and the master's program.

The first stage of the Huasahuasi program was carried out from August 6-26 in 1973. The first week was spent at the university organizing the university group and working out tentative plans. On August 12 the group traveled to Huasahuasi where the community provided the members with food and lodgings for a two-week period. August 13-18 was spent by team members in moving about the community, visiting large and small farms, talking with the farmers about their plans and problems. These activities had the dual purpose of helping team members arrive at tentative diagnoses of the technical and social and economic problems of the community and of interesting community members in participation in the seminar programs being planned for the following week.

On Sunday, August 19, the team members were invited to a general assembly of the community for a presentation and discussion of the program for the following week. During that week, the visiting team held small group meetings in each neighborhood. Each presentation was followed by an open and informal discussion. Officials of the Ministry of Agriculture also participated in the instructional program, and one of them had a particular responsibility to deal with pest control.

In February 1974, with only minor changes in its membership, the team made a return visit to Huasahuasi for another week of intensive discussion with the farmers. At this time the community agreed to establish demonstration fields in each neighborhood so that the farmers could learn through participation farm management practices that would combine the best features of traditional methods with those developed through research. In the introduction of these changes, Moreno feels it is particularly important to avoid disruption of the area's characteristic ecological system of environment-crops-man.

On the agricultural sciences side of the problem, Moreno explores possibilities for establishing continuing linkages between the International Potato Center and the Ministry of Agriculture on the one hand and the community of Huasahuasi on the other, so as to improve the community's access to knowledge and to the material inputs needed for development. He also hopes to establish Huasahuasi as a community field station where new ideas can be tried out under more natural conditions than those prevailing in field stations controlled by a university or a government agency.

The field work yielded information as to the factors enabling some farmers to get far greater yields than others. Studies also revealed the sometimes conflicting and ambiguous influences upon the farmers wielded by employees of the Ministry of Agriculture, ranging from agrarian reform to production and to EPSA, the new marketing organization.

These findings are not novel or unusual. Studies revealed the kinds of social and economic problems that are familiar to any experienced student of rural development, yet the findings are no less important on that account. It is not enough to know what conditions are likely to prevail in the "typical" peasant community. Just as the agricultural scientist needs to have systematic knowledge of the climate and soil conditions, so also does the behavioral scientist need systematic socioeconomic information regarding the particular area where changes are to be introduced.

While it is far too early to evaluate this project in terms of potato production, the strategy pursued seems to be highly significant both in organizational and economic terms. On the organizational side, the project involves building interorganizational collaboration among the university, the Ministry of Agriculture and the International Potato Center, and, at the community level, involving Huasahuasi people in development of plans and in contributing to financial support. Clearly the Huasahuasi people are not simply passive recipients of what the experts decide is good for them.

It is hard to imagine a more fruitful educational experience for both professors and students than this intensive participation with the farmers in the joint effort to improve agriculture in Huasahuasi and, indirectly in other communities. Field trips of similar length yet organized for the sole purpose of advancing the education of students would cost as much while yielding much less learning to students (and professors) and producing no benefits to the farmers.

In other developing countries, programs that have involved a comparable scope of interorganizational collaboration and farmer participation have been built on large-scale government and international financing. The Huasahuasi project has cost little more than the travel expenses to get the team to Huasahuasi and their living expenses in the community (covered by Huasahuasi). To be sure, larger financing will be required if the full potential of the project is to be achieved, but the fact that such promising beginnings could be made on a "shoestring" should encourage development planners elsewhere to believe that they do not have to wait for major grants from governments or foundations before launching their own innovative projects.

5

New Directions
in Social Theory

In *The Structure of Scientific Revolutions*, Thomas Kuhn[21] argues that major advances in the natural sciences have come when an old paradigm is abandoned in favor of a new one. While this shift may appear to come suddenly, it is preceded by a long period in which scientists have tried to elaborate and modify the old paradigm in order to make it compatible with discrepant empirical findings. While it would be exaggerating the precision and systematic qualities of theory in the behavioral sciences to speak of paradigms and paradigm shifts, we are currently witnessing a forward movement of knowledge of this general character. This is especially impressive because, with little communication between specialists studying organizational behavior in industry and those studying the sociology of development, basically the same type of shift in focus and problem definition has been taking place.

What we now call organizational behavior (which has also been called human relations in industry, industrial sociology, formal organizations, etc.) arose out of opposition to scientific management with its emphasis upon formal organization structure and technology. In reacting against the dehumanizing of work and the autocratic di-

rection of workers that seem to flow from that doctrine,
early students of human relations abandoned the study of
formal organization structure, technology and the division
of labor in order to concentrate upon interpersonal relations: the relations among workers or managers in "the informal group," the relations between workers and their
immediate supervisor.

This interest led eventually to what came to be called
"participation management," a vaguely formulated doctrine that was the most popular general theme in management development programs for many years. In its most
popular form, participation management involved interpersonal relations in an economic and technological vacuum. Proponents of this doctrine hoped to find strategies
for improvement of interpersonal relations that would
make it possible to increase the productivity and satisfaction of workers simultaneously. The key to solution of the
problems of human conflict and low productivity lay in
"democratic leadership," a style in which the superior con-
sulted his subordinates as to what should be done and also
involved them in group discussions in advance of management decision making.

Theorists of participation management focused upon
authority or vertical relations between the supervisor and
the supervised, the manager and his subordinates. The
problem was to transform authoritarian leadership into
democratic leadership. This was not to be done through
making basic structural changes in the relations between
superiors and subordinates but rather through a volun-
taristic approach in which superiors recognized they
would get better results both in productivity and satisfaction of their subordinates if they adopted democratic leadership styles. This single-minded concentration on vertical relations involved an almost complete neglect of
horizontal relations among units in the same organization
or between organizations. It also involved a neglect of
technology, work flow and the structuring of work activities, the implicit assumption being that a skillful structuring of interpersonal relations was all that was needed.

The theory of participation management retained its

popularity for so long because it fits so well with the democratic and egalitarian values of American culture. There were indeed empirical studies that seemed to confirm some of the postulates of participation management, but there was also an increasing number of studies with discrepant findings. Finally researchers came to recognize problems of organizational behavior on which participation management threw no light at all.

The reformulation of social theory now underway in this field does not involve an abandonment of humanistic values regarding human dignity and democracy, yet it requires us to examine the conditions for realization of these values by concentrating upon the structural elements influencing human behavior. This means looking at the social system first in terms of technology, work flow, division of labor, structuring of work activities and the system of rewards and penalties (both economic and noneconomic).

While retaining an interest in vertical relations, the new approach focuses upon the structuring of horizontal relations. We now recognize that the modern organization cannot function effectively unless it develops patterns for coordination and cooperation among units that are not subject to the same authority figure. We are also examining systems in which the sharing of power does not depend on the voluntary decision of the administrator but is built into a system involving elements of worker self-management.

In rural community research, there are parallels to the ideology of participation management in the dogmas of community development. This approach also dealt with interpersonal relations in an economic and technological vacuum. As in studies of organizations, the focus was on the authority and decision-making system. It was thought that the "passive peasant"'s resistance to change could be overcome if he became involved in making group decisions.

Community development planners hoped that if one could get people involved in face-to-face discussions of their problems, they would talk their way around power issues. Thus the theorists neglected to deal with power in any systematic way, often ignoring power differentials within the community and between the community and outsiders.

'While students of a community might sometimes give attention to relations between villagers and representatives of outside agencies, they never left the base of the community to study the organizations responsible for providing goods and services to the community or, further, the interrelations of outside organizations having an impact upon rural community life. Technology was not included in community development research but was left to the agricultural engineers. Nor were the students of community development concerned with the nature of the crops or livestock raised and the ways this affected community organization. Agriculture was left to the crop and livestock specialists.

As students of rural development are becoming increasingly aware of the structural barriers to development, the dogmas of the community development literature are passing from the scene. In several parts of the world, agrarian reform programs of various types and degrees of effectiveness focused on problems in the distribution of power and wealth on the countryside.

A new strategy for rural development research is emerging. This involves giving major attention to the social, economic and political problems of irrigation water control, since water is crucial to the success of new technical packages. Behavioral scientists are now recognizing that different crops have different activity requirements and therefore will result in significant differences in social organization. Since economic elements make up a large part of the rewards and penalties motivating farmer behavior, the behavioral scientist is studying credit systems and input and product markets, including the bartering of crops.

The trend is clearly away from studying the community as if it were a self-contained social system. Research is being increasingly focused on linkages among communities and between the community and other organizations. It is difficult to document these trends from the published literature because, so far as I have been able to discover, the main ideas are still scattered among recent publications and no one has as yet undertaken to pull the fragments together. Many of these ideas have emerged out of my discussions with anthropologists, sociologists and economists at Cornell and elsewhere. If these cannot yet be called ideas whose time has come, I see that time arriving in the near future, and it is my hope to hasten its arrival by articulating as systematically as I can the new theoretical orientation I see emerging.

My confidence that this is the way to go is further bolstered by the recognition of convergence of ideas in a third line of research. Political scientists studying "institution building" place major emphasis upon what they call linkages. While Esman[22] uses the term in a broader sense, he clearly states that the capacity of an organization to contribute to the development of its society depends in large measure upon the effectiveness of the interorganizational relations (linkages) it is able to establish and maintain.

While the amount of verified behavioral science knowledge immediately applicable to agricultural development is still disappointingly small, the fact that we have been abandoning unproductive old ways of thinking and that we are developing a more promising theoretical framework provides grounds for optimism. Furthermore, that the same type of quasi-paradigm shift is occurring in studies of organizational behavior, of rural development and of institution building suggests that we may be on the threshhold of important breakthroughs in social knowledge.

As is often said, there is nothing so practical as a good theory. While behavioral scientists are still, in any strict scientific sense, far from a theory of agricultural development, the theoretical framework now emerging should accelerate our progress so that we can join more effectively with agricultural scientists in a joint search for solutions to the problems of food shortages and rural development.

I have argued that organizational systems have been

the major neglected element in research and planning for agricultural development. From this conclusion it follows that the advancement of knowledge on organizational systems can offer major contributions to agricultural development. Nevertheless, let me close with a word of caution. In a field where progress is so desperately needed, there may be a tendency for planners to grasp any new idea and adopt it as *the* answer to their problems. It should be recognized that organizational systems are neutral in relation to the policies they are implementing. Thus when the government planners adopt policies which, consciously or unconsciously, are designed to favor the interests of the more affluent rural people, then the improvement of the organizational systems supporting those policies will maximize the differential and inequitable effects of the green revolution. It is only when government policies and programs are intelligently designed to improve the lot of the rural poor that we can expect improvements in organizational systems to make important contributions to social justice.

Notes

1. The term *behavioral sciences* is generally used to refer to sociology, social anthropology and social psychology. It should be noted that political scientists concerned with studies of political behavior and economists studying economic activities at the micro level of farm or firm could also be covered by the general label of *behavioral scientists*.

2. See John M. Cohen, "Effects of Green Revolution Strategies on Tenants and Small-Scale Landowners in the Chilalo Region of Ethiopia," *Journal of Developing Areas*, April 1975; Francine Frankel, "The Politics of the Green Revolution: Shifting Patterns of Peasant Participation in India and Pakistan," in *Food, Population and Employment: The Impact of the Green Revolution*, ed. Thomas T. Poleman and Donald K. Freebairn (New York: Praeger Publishers, 1973); and Donald K. Freebairn, "Income Disparities in the Agricultural Sector: Regional and Institutional Stresses," in *Food, Population and Employment: The Impact of the Green Revolution*, ed. Thomas T. Poleman and Donald K. Freebairn (New York: Praeger Publishers, 1973).

3. International Rice Research Institute, *Changes in Rice Farming in Selected Asian Countries* (Los Baños, Laguna, Philippines, 1974).

4. Max Millikan and David Hapgood, *No Easy Harvest: The Dilemma of Agriculture in Developing Countries* (Boston: Little, Brown and Co., 1956).

5. William F. Whyte, "Rural Peru—Peasants as Activists," in *Contemporary Culture and Societies of Latin America*, second edition, ed. Dwight Heath (New York: Random House, 1974).

6. Jose Matos Mar et al., *Dominacion Y Cambios en el Peru Rural* (Lima: Instituto de Estudios Peruanos, 1969).

7. James Green, "Success and Failure in Technical Assistance," *Human Organization* 20 (1961): 1.

8. Philip H. Coombs with Manzoor Ahmed, *Attacking Rural Poverty: How Nonformal Education Can Help* (Baltimore: Johns Hopkins University Press, 1974), pp. 43-44.

9. Arthur T. Mosher, *Creating a Progressive Rural Structure* (New York: Agricultural Development Council, 1969).

10. E. B. Rice, *Extension in the Andes: An Evaluation of Official U.S. Assistance to Agricultural Extension Services in Central and South America* (Washington; D.C.: Agency for International Development, 1971).

11. Coombs, *Attacking Rural Poverty*, pp. 238-40.

12. Milton Barnett, personal communication.

13. Randolph Barker, personal communication.

14. William F. Whyte and Lawrence K. Williams, *Toward an Integrated Theory of Development* (Ithaca, N.Y.: New York State School of Industrial and Labor Relations, Cornell University, 1968).

15. *Por y Para La Communidad* (Lima: Ministerio de Industria y Comercio, Direccion General de Communidades Laborales, 1973), p. 25.

16. Coombs, *Attacking Rural Poverty*, p. 205.

17. Benedict Stavis, *Rural Local Governance and Agricultural Development* (Ithaca, New York: Cornell University Center for International Studies, 1971).

18. Coombs, *Attacking Rural Poverty*, p. 115.

19. Ibid., p. 85.

20. Gary Hansen, "Regional Administration for Rural Development in Indonesia: The Bimas Case," *Honolulu: East-West Center*, Working Paper Series No. 26, 1972.

21. Thomas Kuhn, *The Structure of Scientific Revolutions* (Chicago: University of Chicago Press, 1962).

22. Milton Esman, "The Elements of Institution Building," in *Institution Building and Development*, ed. Joseph W. Eaton (Beverly Hills and London: Sage Publications, 1972).